Rebecca Hunter
Photography by Chris Fairclough

Evans

Published in paperback by Evans Brothers Ltd in 2004
2A Portman Mansions
Chiltern Street
London W1U 6NR
England

First published in 2000. Reprinted 2005

Hunter, Rebecca
My first day at school, - (First Times)
1. First day of school - Juvenile literature
I. Title
372

ISBN 0 237 52693 X

Acknowledgements
Planning and production by Discovery Books
Editor: Rebecca Hunter
Photographer: Chris Fairclough
Designer: Ian Winton
Consultant: Trevor Jellis M.A., M.Phil., A.F.B.Ps., Psychol. is a Chartered Psychologist who has spent thirty years working with individuals, schools, companies and major corporate institutions in the management of stress. He deals with individuals who are suffering from stress both in their family and in the workplace.

The publishers would like to thank Roshaurn Lee, Dionne Waite, Mrs Gardner and the staff and pupils of Harborne Infants School, Birmingham for their help in the preparation of this book.

Contents

Today is my first day at school.

Today is my first day at infant school. Mum takes me to school. My little sister comes too.

Mrs Gardner is my new teacher.

My new teacher is Mrs Gardner. She shows me where the toilets are and where to hang my coat. I say goodbye to Mum.

We go to assembly.

My teacher takes me to assembly. All the children sit down in a big room. The headteacher tells us a story from a book.

This is my new classroom.

This is my new classroom. The room is full of other children. I hope they like me.

Mrs Gardner gives us some paper.

I sit down with the children.
Mrs Gardner gives us all some
paper and crayons.
She asks me what I
am going to draw.

I draw a giraffe.

I draw my favourite animal. It is a giraffe. Mrs Gardner pins our pictures on the wall.

We go out to play.

At half past ten we go out to play in the playground.
We play games and run around.
This is my new friend Harprit.

Emily shows me the computer.

After playtime a girl called Emily shows me how to draw on the computer. I have never used a computer before. It is fun.

It is time for lunch.

It is lunchtime. I follow the other children to the dining room. We get in the queue. I am worried I won't like the food.

I sit down with my lunch.

When I am given my lunch I find a place to sit down. A teacher helps me cut it up.

Mrs Gardner reads us a story.

After lunch we sit down to listen to Mrs Gardner. She reads us a story from a big book.

We look at the books in pairs.

Now we have our own books.

We look at the books in pairs.

Harprit can read some of the words. I look at the pictures.

I build a tower.

Next we have free play.
We can choose what to do. I am building a tower out of bricks.

It's time to go home.

It is time to go home. Mum is waiting outside for me.

I tell her about the computer and playing with Harprit. I think I'm going to like school.

Index

Notes to Parents and Teachers

The first day at school is full of new and sometimes unwelcome experiences. Being one of a large crowd, taking turns, learning new routines and rules, and having to be with strangers for most of the day can all be stressful experiences for young children. Children may feel that they have been rejected from home, especially if there is a younger child still there. Children may feel very self-conscious in a new large group, especially if they have not been to playgroups or nurseries beforehand. Children who are more confident may feel resentful if they do not have an adult's full attention.

Much can be done beforehand to prepare children for their first day at school. Visiting the school either informally or at a familiarisation event can be very helpful. The child should become used to sitting quietly and listening to a parent before they go to school so that this does not seem a strange thing to do when at school. Parents should show great interest in what the child has done during the school day but not be upset if the child cannot remember every detail. Where there are younger children in the family, they should be included in discussions about school, so that no one feels left out.

- Teachers can help by explaining routines and rules as simply as possible.

- The location of the toilet should be one of the first pieces of information given to a new child.

- Movement within the larger area of the school should be gently phased in by teaching staff.

- Take a younger brother or sister along to the school entrance on the first day to share the experience.